The Oxford Book of
Choral Music by
Black Composers

Compiled and edited by Marques L. A. Garrett

OXFORD
UNIVERSITY PRESS

OXFORD
UNIVERSITY PRESS

Great Clarendon Street, Oxford OX2 6DP,
United Kingdom

Oxford University Press is a department of the University of Oxford.
It furthers the University's objective of excellence in research, scholarship,
and education by publishing worldwide. Oxford is a registered trade mark of
Oxford University Press in the UK and in certain other countries

First published 2023

Impression: 1

ISBN 978–0–19–356100–7 (paperback)
ISBN 978–0–19–356101–4 (wiro)

Music origination by Andrew Jones
Text origination by Katie Johnston
Printed in Great Britain on acid-free paper by
Halstan & Co. Ltd, Amersham, Bucks.

FOREWORD

Most, if not all, significant moments of social injustice spark a new movement in music to express opinions, to attempt to right an injustice, or to encourage others in the fight for that justice. After the death of George Floyd in May 2020 and the growth of the Black Lives Matter movement, musicians began to increase their search for classical music written by composers of African descent. The arrangements of spirituals were already a popular part of the choral repertoire and remain so. Unfortunately, little was known about the non-idiomatic compositions of Black composers, although these composers have been writing such works for centuries. Racism expressed itself even in the classical music world, with Black composers seldom allowed to play a leading role. It was in 1996 that the ceiling was broken and George Walker won the Pulitzer Prize in Music.

Today it is thrilling to observe the renewed interest from conductors hoping to perform more music by women, Black composers, and other marginalized groups.

The creation of this unique anthology, curated by Dr Marques L. A. Garrett, will undoubtedly assist conductors in learning this exceptional music by Black composers. It comprises works from the sixteenth century through to the twenty-first century and is representative, including music by both Black men and Black women from a variety of nations.

Dr Garrett graduated from Hampton University, where his love of this music was nurtured. It was there that a fire was lit for him, and his quest to discover as much of this music as possible began. This love and passion continued through his master's degree course at the University of North Carolina in Greensboro. He collected yet more repertoire during his doctoral studies at Florida State University and has become a leading scholar in this area, presenting sessions on this topic at conferences throughout the United States and abroad.

Perusing the composers and compositions featured in the collection, some names will be familiar, and perhaps it will be discovered that their ethnicity was never revealed. Included are composers who have not only written choral music, but also symphonic compositions, opera, and chamber music. Carlos Simon—one of the younger composers in this anthology—is a perfect example. In 2021, he was appointed as a composer-in-residence at the Kennedy Center, writing symphonic music and opera. Other examples of composers with extended compositions include Ulysses Kay, Julia Perry, and Leslie Adams.

This collection is an excellent introduction to this often-overlooked music. I hope that it not only allows the user to have a look at the works within its covers, but also encourages the exploration of other repertoire written by the composers included within.

DR ANDRÉ J. THOMAS
Associate Artist with the London Symphony Orchestra
National President of the American Choral Directors Association
Professor Emeritus, Florida State University

This collection is dedicated to the memory of Royzell L. Dillard, Assistant Professor of Music and Director of University Choirs at Hampton University. During my undergraduate education, he sparked in me the curiosity to explore the wealth of choral music by Black composers.
—MLAG

CONTENTS

In order to minimize page turns, some pieces have been placed out of alphabetical order.

Many of the pieces in this collection are available separately in print or as a digital download.

INTRODUCTION

Composers such as Harry T. Burleigh, William Grant Still, Florence Price, and their predecessors were among the early generation of musicians whose compositions set the standard for both breadth and depth of choral music by Black* composers. Despite the work of such trailblazers, the music of Black composers too often existed both in the shadows of that of their non-Black counterparts and of the idiomatic genres—spirituals, gospel, and jazz—associated with Black musicians.

A quick perusal of established choral collections from the twentieth and early twenty-first centuries reveals the lack of diversity—geographic region aside—among the featured composers, with many whose accomplishments were recognized in their lifetimes absent from these publications. Missing, for example, is José Maurício Nunes Garcia, who was and is still known throughout Brazil for his priesthood and musical contributions to the Roman Catholic Church. Samuel Coleridge-Taylor is shockingly absent from several books, despite his success being documented by the hundreds of performances and numerous copies sold of *Hiawatha's Wedding Feast* during the early twentieth century. Likewise, although R. Nathaniel Dett's education included studies at Harvard University, the institution—by all known accounts—did not perform his prize-winning *Don't Be Weary, Traveler* until 101 years after he won their Francis Boott Prize, in 1920.

Racism and social hierarchies are among the contributing factors to the suppression of and lack of exposure for these composers. Of course, this under-representation neither diminishes nor reflects the quality of the contributions of composers of African descent from around the world. Moreover, though many of their names and works were unknown in wider musical circles, the music of these composers was and continues to be a staple part of the repertoire of choirs at Historically Black Colleges and Universities.† Currently, musicians are working to remedy actions of the past by rediscovering music that never received proper recognition.

This anthology was compiled with the following goals in mind:
1. To highlight the contributions of composers of African descent to the choral repertoire
2. To include representative examples of various genres from across the eras of music history
3. To provide a collection for conductors to peruse works by familiar and less-familiar composers
4. To offer a resource for choral literature classes, music education curricula, college/university libraries, personal collections, and more.

The composers in this collection are from Brazil, Canada, Portugal, the United Kingdom, and the United States, although most are of American heritage as a result of their choral output and familiarity among musicians. The historical composers represent the Renaissance, Classical, and Romantic eras in addition to the early twentieth century. The music from the twentieth and twenty-first centuries includes sixteen living composers, and there has been intentional inclusion of works by male and female composers. The thirteen secular and twenty-two liturgical texts span a breadth of repertoire including anthems, choral art songs, madrigals, motets, and part-songs. Limitations to the anthology's scope result from copyright restrictions and availability of manuscripts.

Additional composers for readers to research include, but are not limited to: Kevin Allen; T. J. Anderson; Margaret Bonds; Roland Carter; Noel DaCosta; Rollo Dilworth; Marvin V. Curtis; Mark Fax; Chiquinha Gonzaga; Victor C. Johnson; Hannah Kendall; Shavon Lloyd; Hannibal Lokumbe; Phillip McIntyre; José Joaquim Emérico Lobo de Mesquita; Reginald Nathaniel Parker; Zenobia Powell Perry; Rosephanye Powell; Noah Ryder; Hale Smith; Mitchell Southall; André J. Thomas; George Walker; Mervyn Warren; and Diane White-Clayton.

---

* The term Black is used as a hypernym for any person of the African diaspora.
† An HBCU is '…any historically black college or university that was established prior to 1964, whose principal mission was, and is, the education of black Americans, and that is accredited by a nationally recognized accrediting agency or association determined by the Secretary [of Education] to be a reliable authority as to the quality of training offered or is, according to such an agency or association, making reasonable progress toward accreditation' according to the amended US Higher Education Act of 1965.

While the music in this anthology represents the contributions of Black composers, it does not limit the identity of its performers. This music was made available for people of all ethnicities and backgrounds and not only those of African descent.

Editorial practice

Details of the sources consulted during the preparation of this collection may be found in the commentary. No source has been listed when the work is by a living composer and has not been published prior to this anthology. Where possible, composers were consulted when preparing these editions of their works, and editors are listed for pieces where significant changes were made due to unclear expressive markings or pitch or rhythm discrepancies between the voice and rehearsal piano parts in the source, as well as for new editions of historical works.

Brackets have not been used for editorial dynamics, expressions, breath marks, missing ties, or other markings, as this anthology is intended as a performing edition rather than as a source of critical editions. Editorial metronome markings have been added, however, and are given in square brackets. In line with house style, several scores have additional dynamics at the end of hairpins for clarity. Absent dynamics were added without comment to voice parts when they are present in other voice or instrumental parts. Educated guesses and best practices were considered for the few pitch and rhythm variants and are listed in the commentary. Where applicable, keyboard reductions have been provided for rehearsal use only and are presented in their most readable and playable form. Translations for non-English texts can be found in the commentary to assist choirs in their interpretation. Following house style, UK spellings have been adopted, except in works where the author or composer has used US spellings in their original texts.

In Lusitano's *Emendemus in melius*, italic text indicates editorial underlay for neumes without text. Ligatures from the source have been retained, while barlines and a modern time signature have been added in light of standard contemporary performance practice. *Musica ficta* is incorporated in the keyboard reduction without qualification. Editorial dynamics and syllabic slurs are not included, in accordance with standard early music practice.

Acknowledgements

I am deeply indebted to and wish to thank several people who helped to make this project a reality. I am appreciative of the following people who provided direct contact as I prepared this project. In my research pre-dating the commencement of the anthology, Jennifer B. Lee (Rare Book & Manuscript Library, Columbia University) assisted with contacting the family of Edward Margetson, allowing me to access his music. Heidi Marshall (Center for Black Music Research, Columbia College Chicago) provided access to the James Furman manuscript, while Brenda Nelson-Strauss and William R. Vanden Dries (Archives of African American Music and Culture, Indiana University, Bloomington) provided access to the Charles Coleman collection. Mark Lawson (ECS Publishing) was instrumental in gaining contact with the John Work estate, and my thanks to David von Behren, who assisted with organ registrations. I'm grateful for the emotional support of several colleagues, friends, and loved ones who either talked me through the process or reviewed several iterations of background information on composers and works. They include Vinroy D. Brown, Jr.; Edryn J. Coleman; Alex T. Favazza, Jr.; Derrick Fox; Paula Harper; Nathan Mertens; Jessica Nápoles; Jason D. Thompson; and Khyle Wooten. Finally, André J. Thomas was my major professor at Florida State University who both challenged and supported me in my musical and research pursuits, including my desire to continue championing the choral music of Black composers.

MARQUES L. A. GARRETT
November 2022

Hosanna to the Son of David

Adapted from Matthew 21: 8–9
and Mark 11: 8–10

H. LESLIE ADAMS

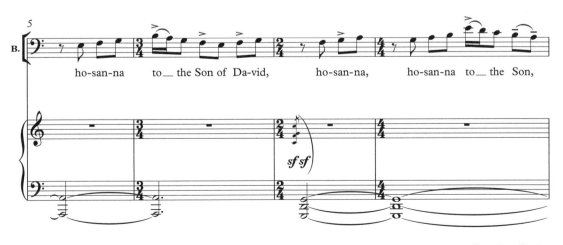

Duration: 3 mins

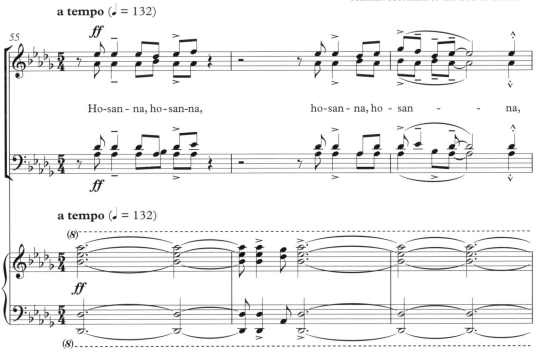

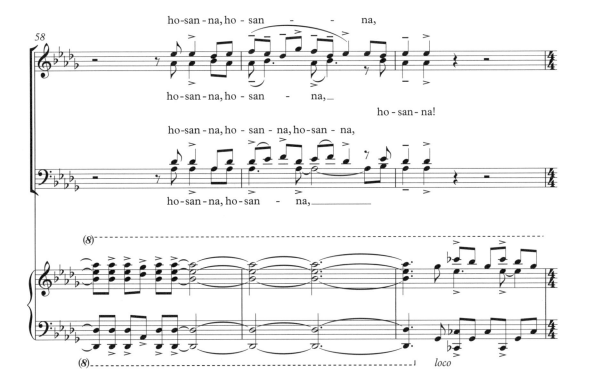

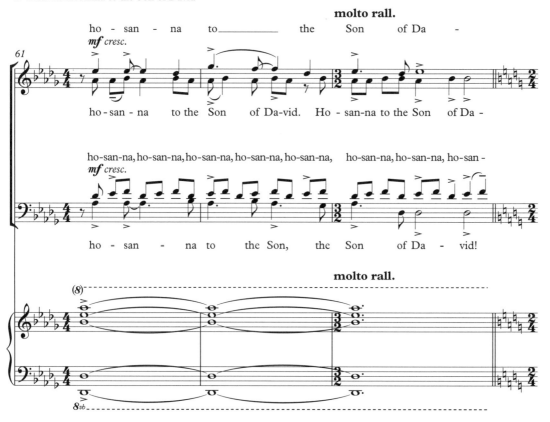

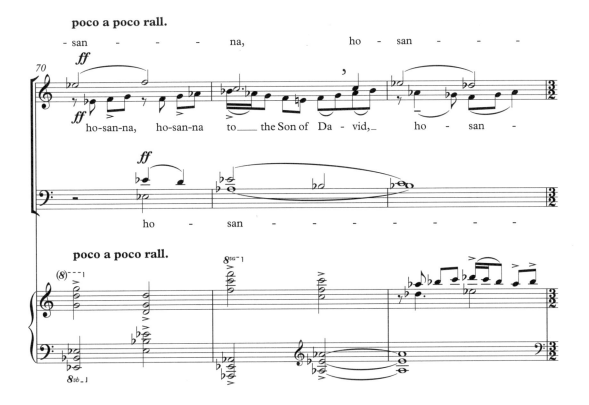

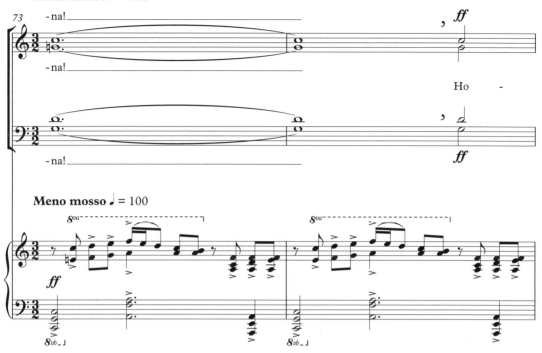

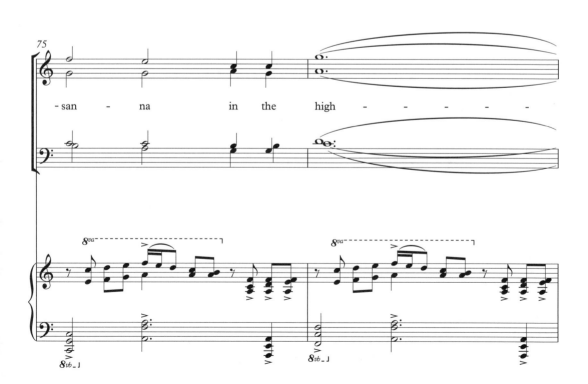

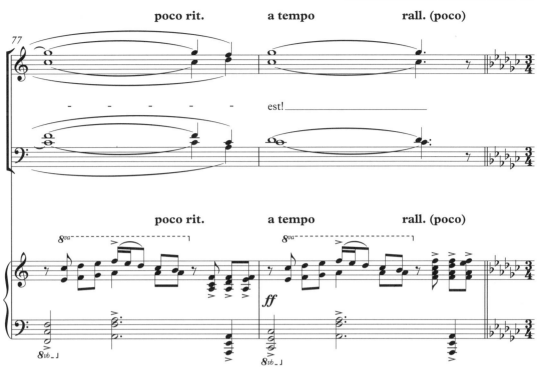

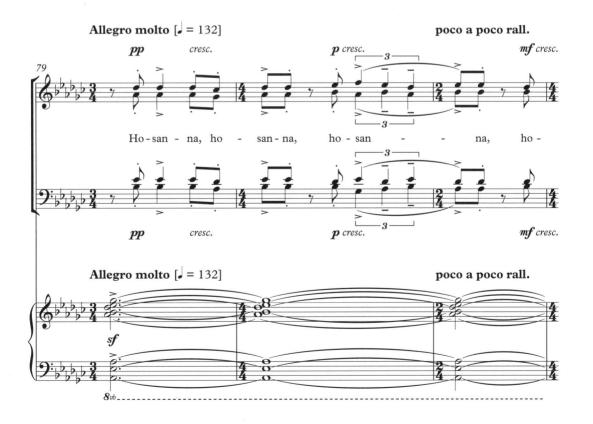

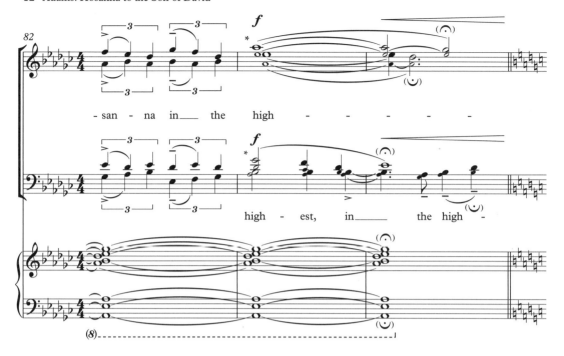

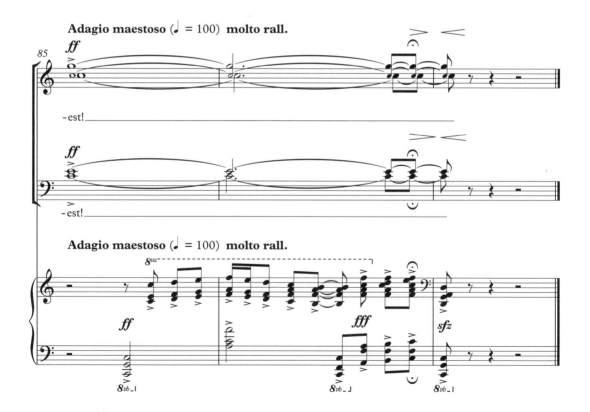

* Small notes in bars/measures 83–4 denote an optional alternative ending and should not be sung as a divisi. If performing the alternative ending, however, the small notes in bars/measures 85–7 may be sung as an optional divisi.

Music of Life

George Parsons Lathrop
(1851–98)

B. E. BOYKIN

Lilting ♩. = 60

Mu-sic is in all grow-ing things; And un-der-neath the silk-y wings

Of small-est in-sects there is stirred A pulse of air that must be heard.

Also available in a version for SSA and piano (ISBN 978–0–19–356167–0).

Duration: 3 mins

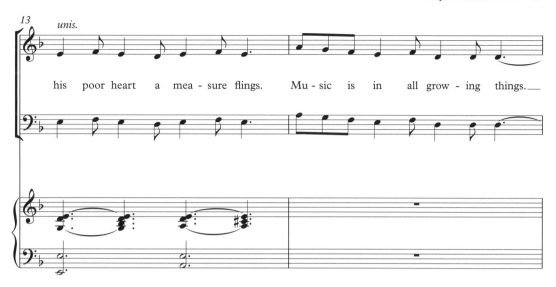

his poor heart a mea - sure flings. Mu - sic is in all grow - ing things.__

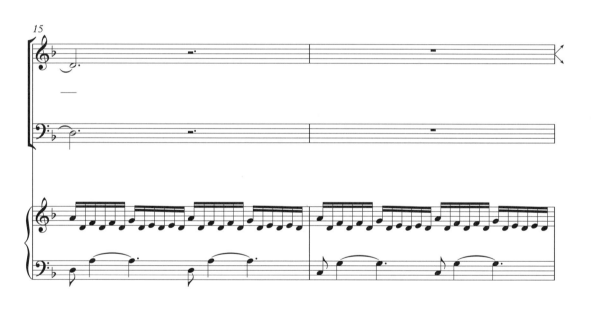

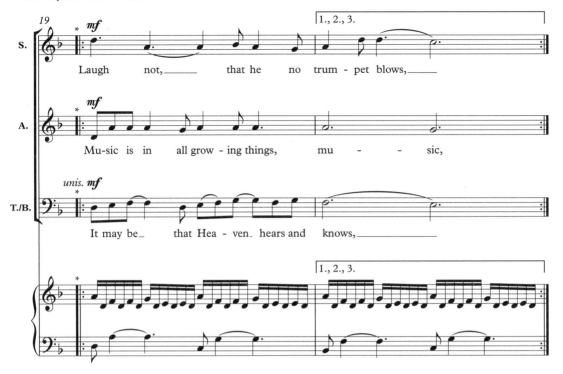

* Starting with sopranos, introduce each voice part one at a time, one after the other, allowing each part to sing their section at least twice. Next, all groups should sing together, repeating the section three times before taking the fourth-time bar/measure.

lis - ten - ings.____ Mu - sic, mu - sic is

lis - ten - ings.____ Mu - sic, mu - sic is

lis - ten - ings.____ Mu - sic, mu - sic is

in____ all liv - ing things._____

in____ all liv - ing things._____

in____ all liv - ing things._____

commissioned by the Episcopal Diocese of Atlanta, Council on Liturgy and Music

O praise the Lord

Psalm 117 (King James Version)

UZEE BROWN, JR.

Duration: 5 mins

to Dr Jason Max Ferdinand and The Jason Max Ferdinand Singers

A Prayer

Paul Laurence Dunbar
(1872–1906)

KEN BURTON

Duration: 4.5 mins

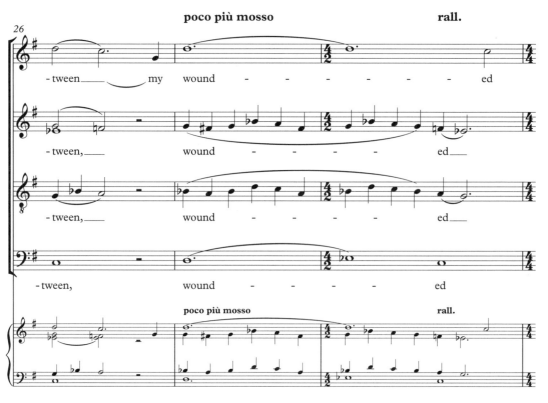

* ⚬⚬⚬ = vibrato

a tempo

feet and God. Where heal - ing wa - ters

flow, do thou my foot - steps lead. My

The 100th Psalm

Psalm 100 (King James Version) (altd)

CHARLES D. COLEMAN
(1929–91)

Duration: 3.5 mins

MEZZO-SOPRANO or TENOR SOLO

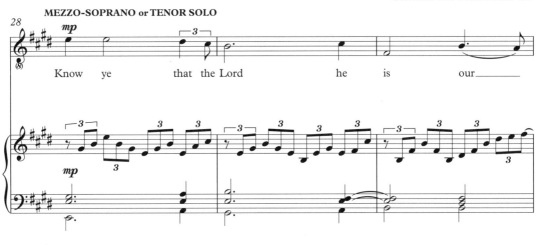

Know ye that the Lord he is our_____

God. It is he that hath made_____ us and

not we our-selves. We are his

⊕ CODA

lands.   Make a joy - ful noise un - to the Lord   and   read   his ho - ly___

word   and   bless his ho - ly___ name, all ye   lands,_ all_ ye__ lands.

in loving memory of my dear sister, Ivorynetta Butler

Dona nobis pacem

From the Ordinary of the Mass

MARK BUTLER

This piece may alternatively be performed in the key of B major.

Duration: 5 mins

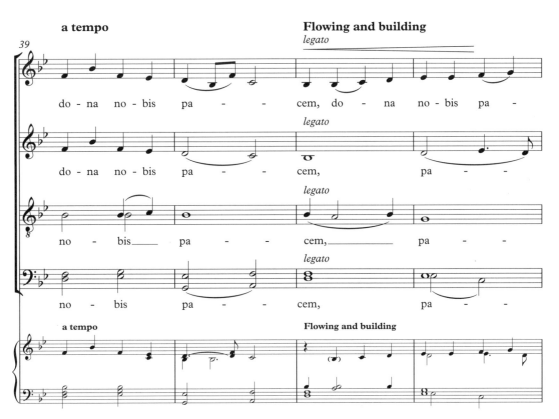

Psalm 131

Psalm 131 (King James Version)

NATHAN CARTER
(1936–2004)

Duration: 2.5 mins

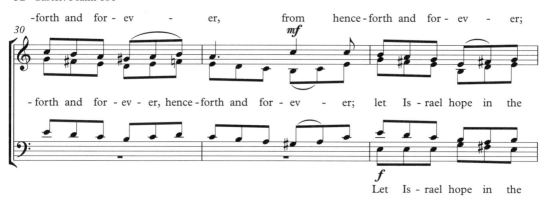

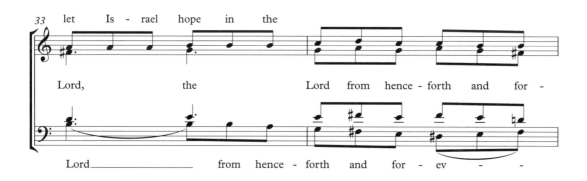

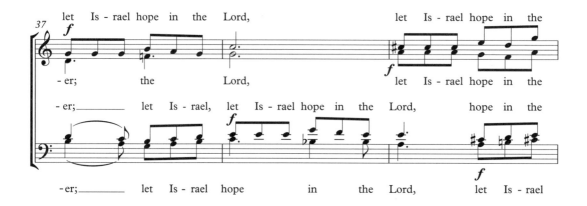

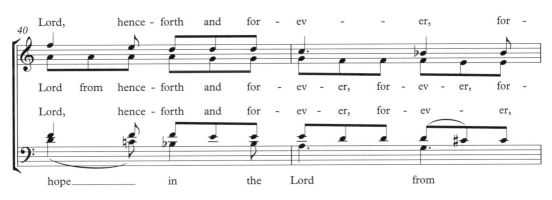

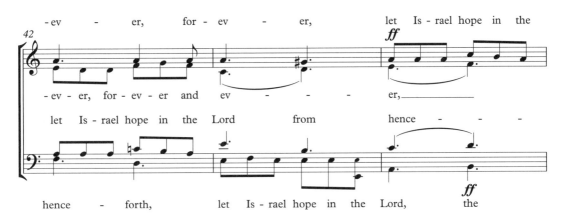

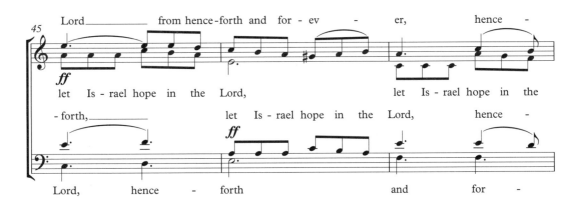

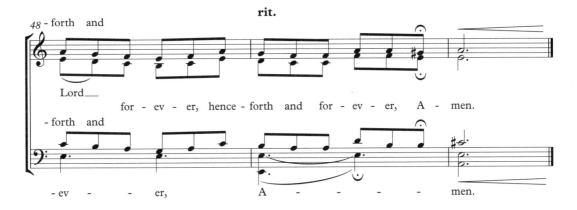

By the lone seashore

Text by Charles Mackay
(1812–89)

SAMUEL COLERIDGE-TAYLOR
(1875–1912)
ed. Marques L. A. Garrett

Duration: 4 mins

The Lord is my strength

Psalm 118: 14, 17 and
J. M. Neale (1818–66)

SAMUEL COLERIDGE-TAYLOR
(1875–1912)
ed. Marques L. A. Garrett

Duration: 4.5 mins

to the Oberlin Music Union, Oberlin, OH, Dr George Whitfield Andrews, conductor

Son of Mary

Henry Hart Milman
(1791–1868)

R. NATHANIEL DETT
(1882–1943)
ed. Marques L. A. Garrett

Duration: 6 mins

Un poco più mosso [♩ = 80]

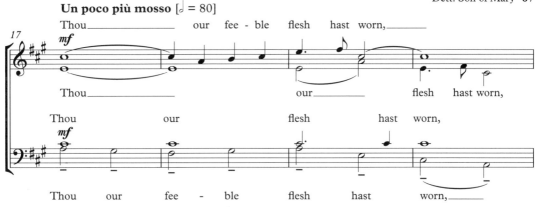

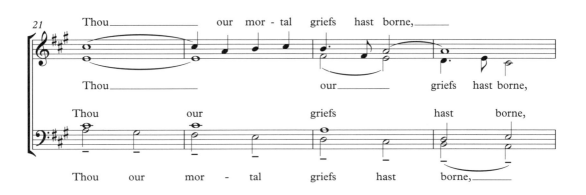

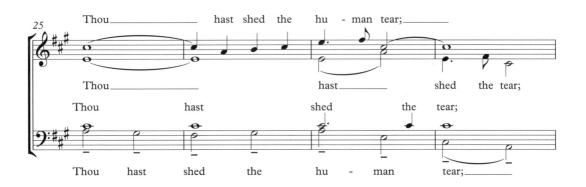

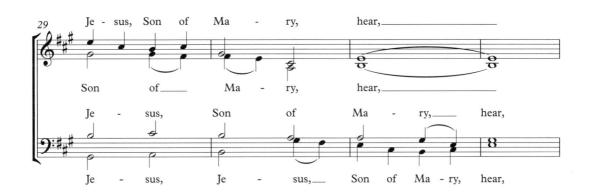

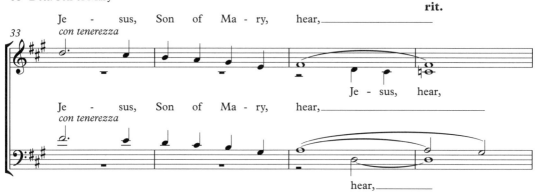

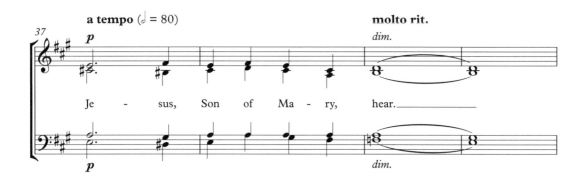

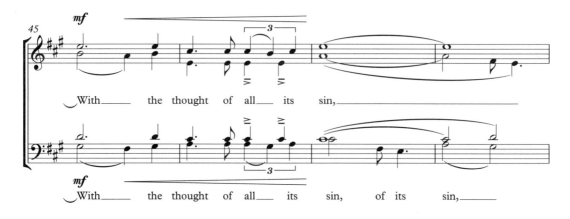

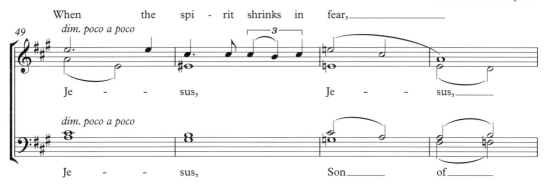

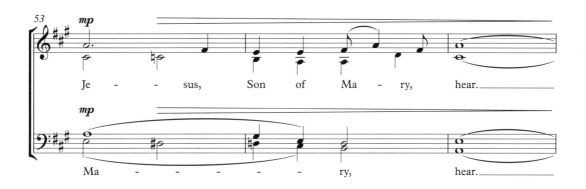

Ben ritmico e largamente [♩ = 60]

Son of Ma - ry, hear. When our eyes grow dim in

death, When we heave the part - ing breath, When our

so - lemn doom is near, Je - sus, Son of Ma - ry, hear.

Un poco marcato ed animato [♩ = 84]

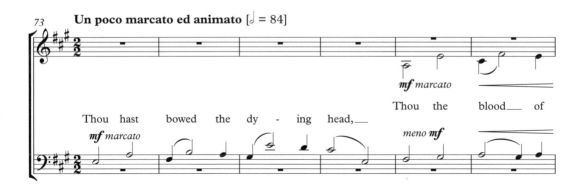

Thou hast bowed the dy - ing head,___ Thou the blood___ of

* Composer originally set 'human', but changed here to 'mortal' in line with Henry Hart Milman's text. This is the only time that 'human' is used instead of 'mortal'.

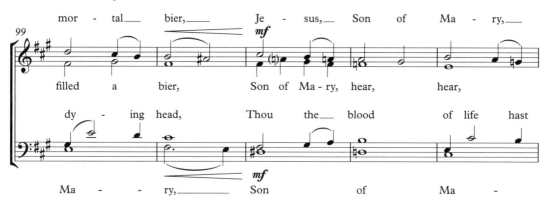

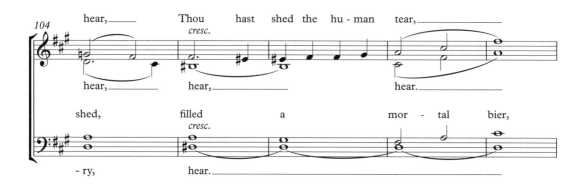

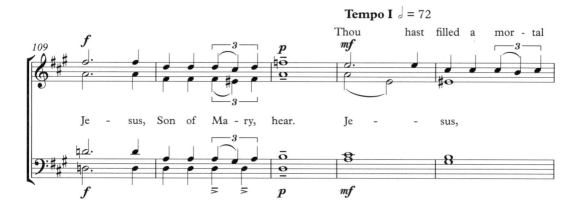

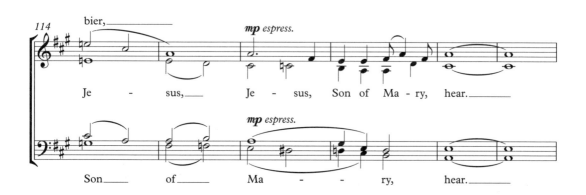

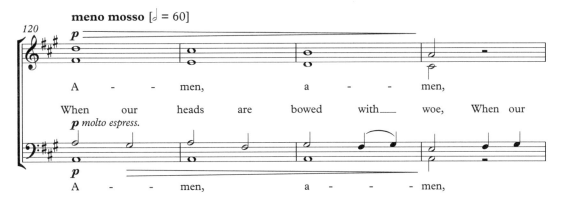

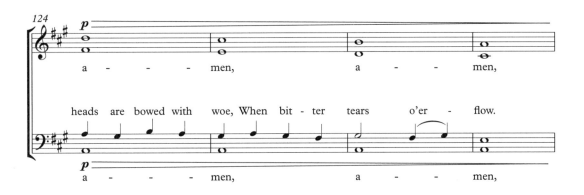

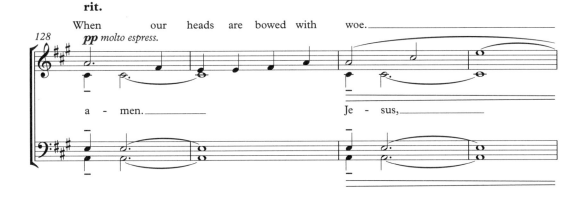

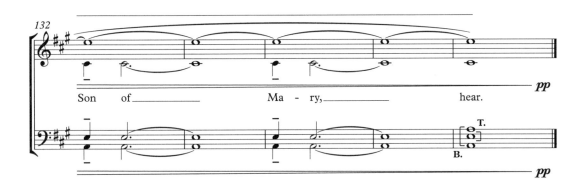

in loving memory of my Aunt Permelia Hansbrough

Four Little Foxes

Lew Sarett
(1888–1954)

JAMES FURMAN
(1937–89)

1. Speak gently

Duration: 3.5 mins

2. Walk softly

3. Go lightly

4. Step softly

Ave maris stella

Vesper hymn, c.9th century

JOSÉ MAURÍCIO NUNES GARCIA
(1767–1830)
ed. Marques L. A. Garrett and Alec Schumacker
orchestral reduction by Alec Schumacker

Duration: 1.5 mins

Alleluia, angelus Domini

Feast of the Holy Innocents
From Matthew 2: 13–14

JOSÉ MAURÍCIO NUNES GARCIA
(1767–1830)
ed. Marques L. A. Garrett
orchestral reduction by Alec Schumacker

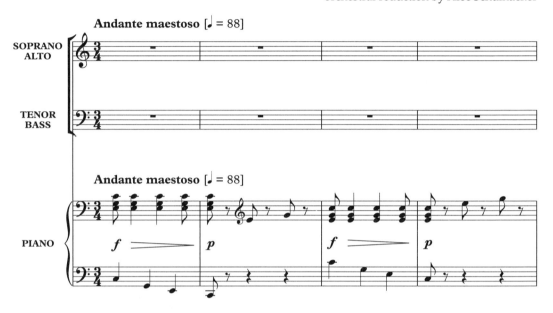

Duration: 3 mins

to Dr Anthony Trecek-King for his concerts with Seraphic Fire

My heart be brave

James Weldon Johnson
(1871–1938)

MARQUES L. A. GARRETT

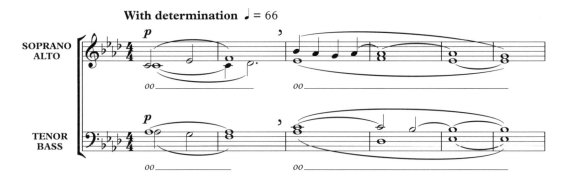

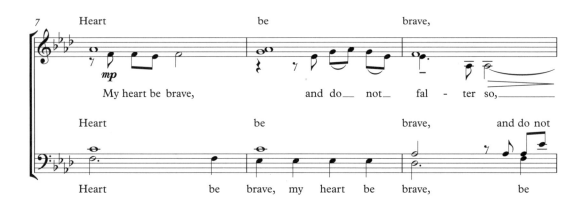

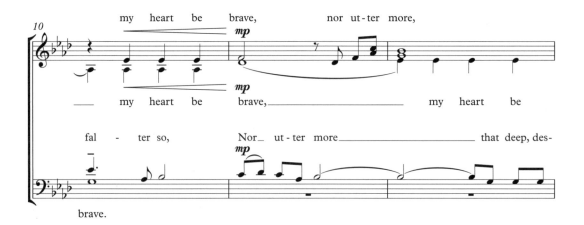

Also available in a version for TTBB (ISBN 978–0–19–356080–2).

Duration: 4 mins

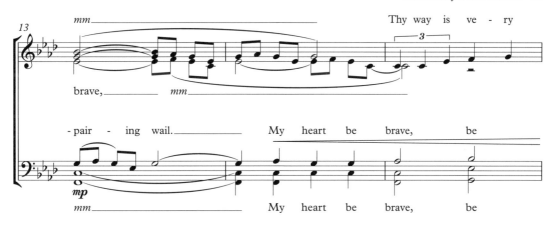

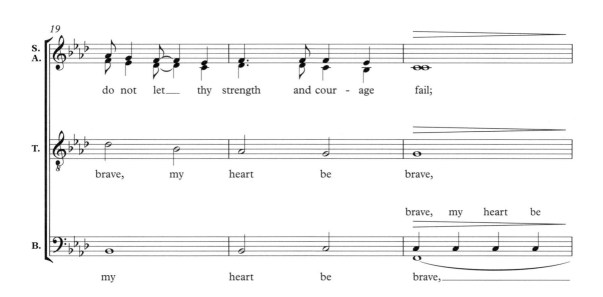

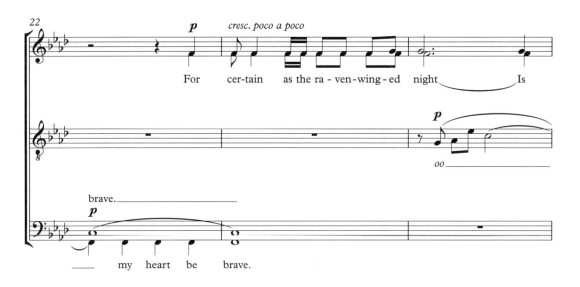

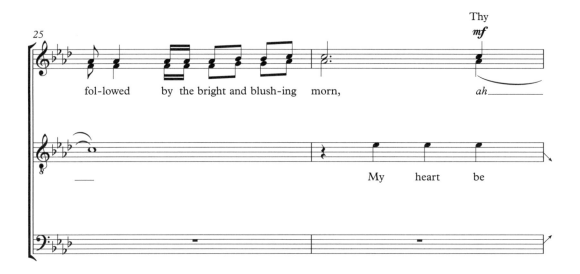

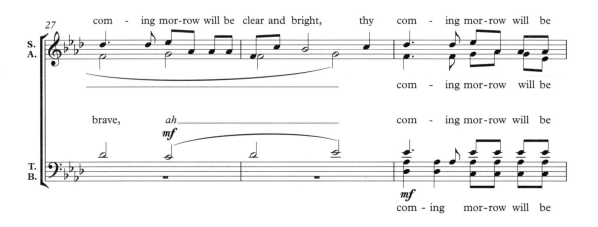

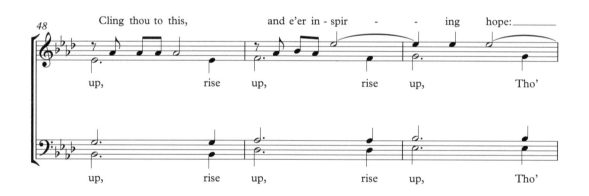

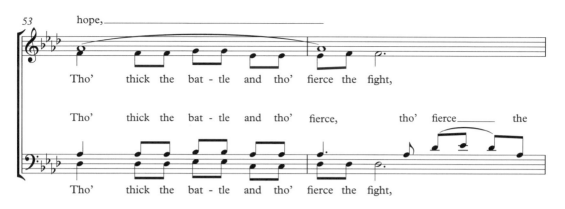

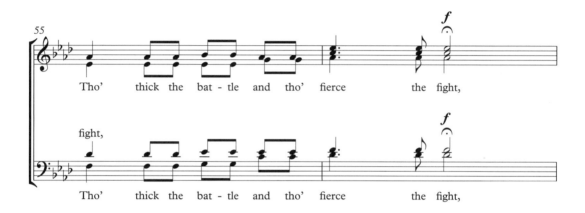

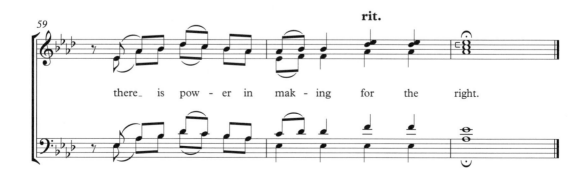

Commissioned by Trinity Episcopal, Portland, May 2021

The Gift to Sing

James Weldon Johnson
(1871–1938)

DAMIEN GETER

Duration: 4 mins

God be merciful

Psalm 67: 1–4 (King James Version)

ADOLPHUS HAILSTORK

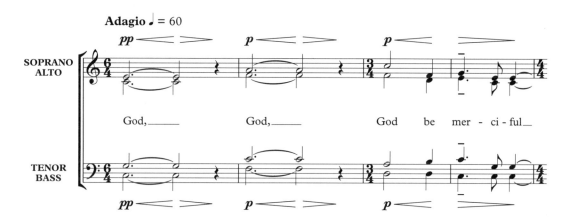

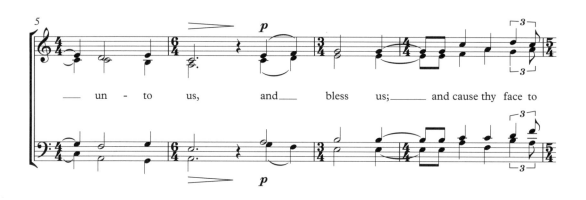

Duration: 2.5 mins

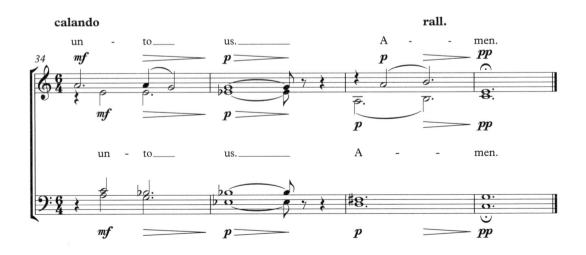

for Adavion Wayne and the Dekaney High School Chorale, Spring ISD, Houston, Texas

Bring me all your dreams

Langston Hughes
(1902–67)

CHRISTOPHER H. HARRIS

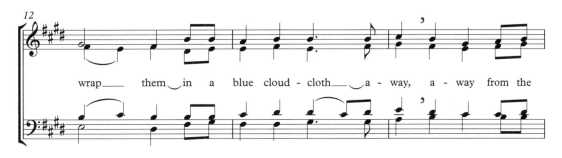

Duration: 4 mins

* Smaller notes should be sung by a few voices.

Commissioned by the Milwaukee Choristers, James Benjamin Kinchen, Jr., conductor

April Rain Song

Langston Hughes
(1902–67)

ROBERT A. HARRIS

Duration: 3 mins

for the Williamsport, Pennsylvania, Area High School Concert Chorale,
Janet Herrick, Conductor

Oh, how can I keep from singing?

Text unattributed

ROBERT A. HARRIS

Duration: 3.5 mins

Ecce sacerdos magnus

Mode 8 plainsong responsory
for the reception of a bishop (Liber Usualis)

DAVID HURD

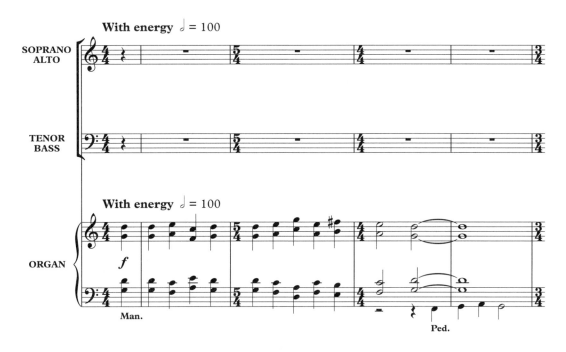

Duration: 5.5 mins

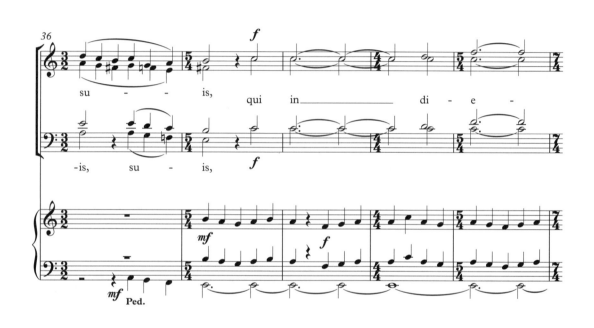

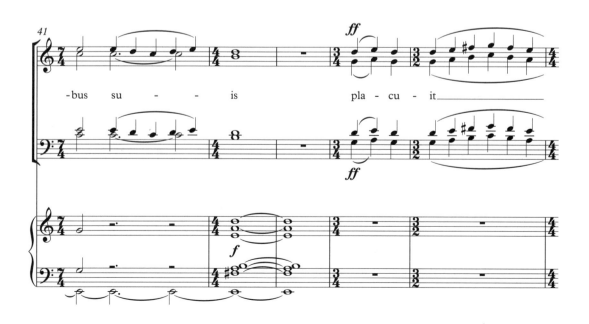

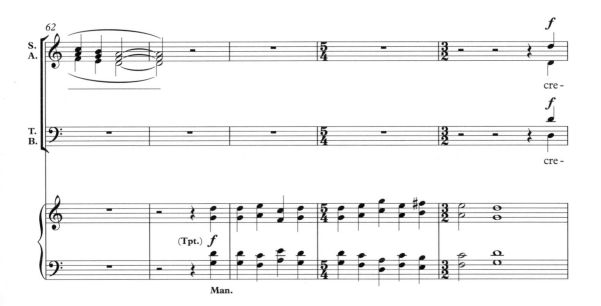

for the Dickinson College Choir

As Joseph was a-walking

Trad. English

ULYSSES KAY
(1917–95)

Duration: 3 mins

to David Randolph and The Randolph Singers

How stands the glass around?

James Wolfe
(1727–59)

ULYSSES KAY
(1917–95)

Duration: 3.5 mins

Dedicated to the Brazeal Dennard Chorale

Psalm 57

Psalm 57: 1, 7, 10–11

BETTY JACKSON KING
(1928–94)

Duration: 6.5 mins

Emendemus in melius

Responsory for Ash Wednesday/the First Sunday of Lent

VICENTE LUSITANO
(*c.*1520–*c.*1561)
ed. Marques L. A. Garrett

For more information about *musica ficta* (small accidentals above the stave), please see the Commentary.
The employment of *musica ficta* is at the discretion of the performers.

Duration: 4.5 mins

A few more years shall roll

Horatius Bonar
(1808–89)

EDWARD MARGETSON
(1891–1962)

Duration: 4 mins

to Howard Swanson

In Celebration

Langston Hughes
(1902–67)

DOROTHY RUDD MOORE
(1940–2022)

Duration: 6 mins

for the Winston-Salem State University Choir, North Carolina,
James Benjamin Kinchen, Jr., Director

I, too

Langston Hughes (1902–67)

UNDINE SMITH MOORE
(1904–89)

Duration: 4.5 mins

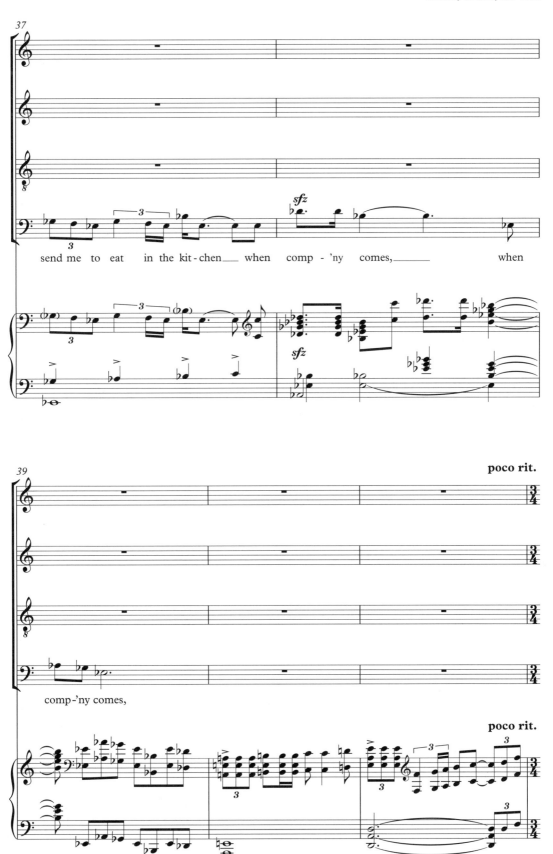

* Cue-sized notes indicate that Tenors may optionally join Basses.

to my brother, The Rev. B. J. Johnson, III, Atlanta, Ga.

See what love

1 John 3: 1, 3 (altd)

LENA J. McLIN

* fermata: 2nd time only.

Duration: 2.5 mins

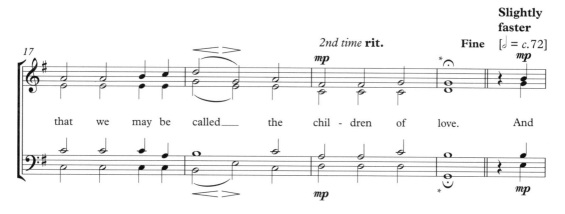

* fermata: 2nd time only—hold for three ♩ beats.

to the Hampton Institute Choir, Hampton, Virginia

Song of our Savior

Words and music by
JULIA PERRY
(1924–79)

Duration: 4 mins

Resignation

Words and music by
FLORENCE PRICE
(1887–1953)

Duration: 2.5 mins

* Optional divisi.

Sanctus

Text from the Ordinary of the Mass

CARLOS SIMON

* Singers should whisper 'Sanctus' at random throughout bars/measures 3 and 4.

Duration: 3 mins

Magnificat

Luke 1: 46–55

ZANAIDA STEWART ROBLES

This is a movement of the complete work *Magnificat and Nunc Dimittis*, which is available in two scorings: SATB and organ (ISBN 978–0–19–356507–4) and SATB with piano and organ (ISBN 978–0–19–356329–2).

Duration: 5.5 mins

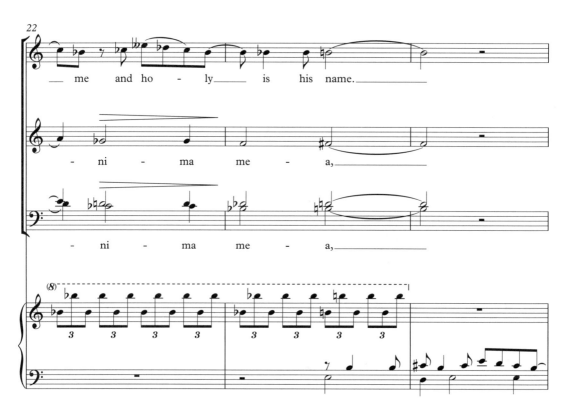

*This passage may be played an octave lower, as required.

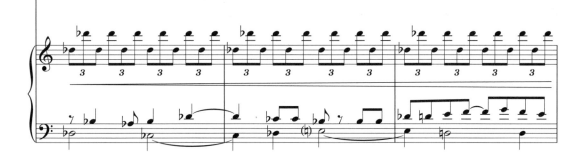

He hath fill - ed the hun - gry with good things___

___ and the rich he hath sent emp - ty___ a - way.___

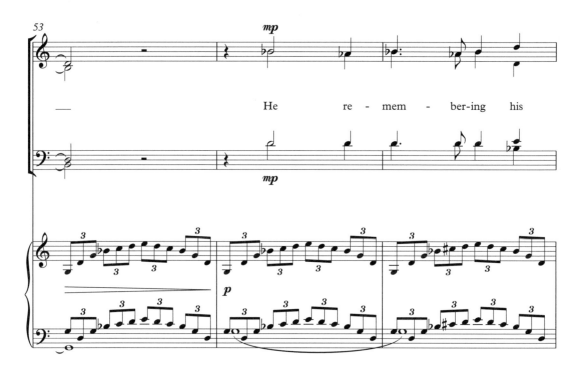

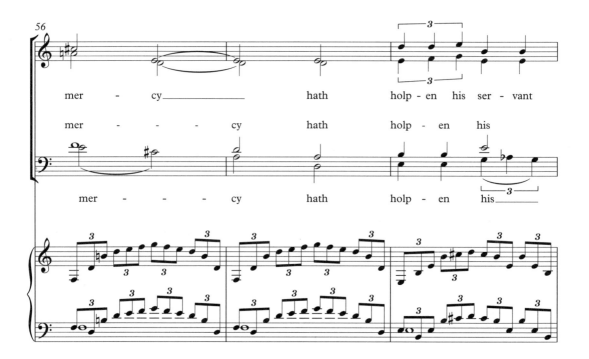

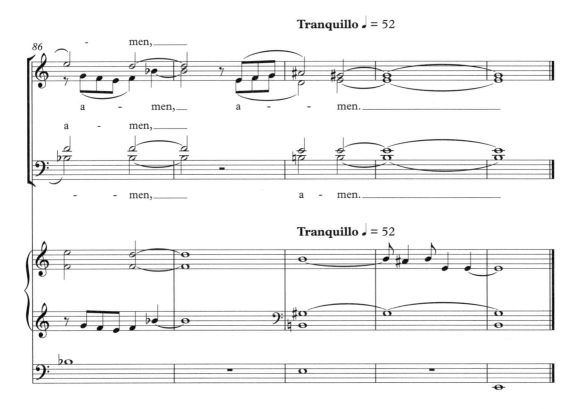

to St Mark's Episcopal Church, Charleston, SC

Rivers of Living Water

John 7: 37–8

TREVOR WESTON

Commissioned by the American Guild of Organists 2003 Region IV Convention for performance in Charleston, South Carolina, churches on Pentecost, 8 June 2003.

Duration: 4.5 mins

* Basses may sing at the lower octave, if required.

to Van S. Whitted, Organist of St Mark's Methodist Church, New York

The sun himself shall fade

GALLAGHER
from The Old South Church Hymnal

JOHN W. WORK III
(1901–67)

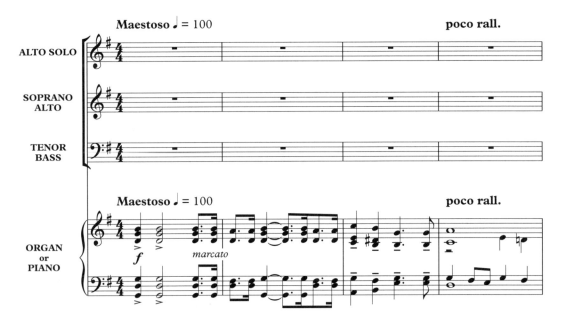

Duration: 2.5 mins

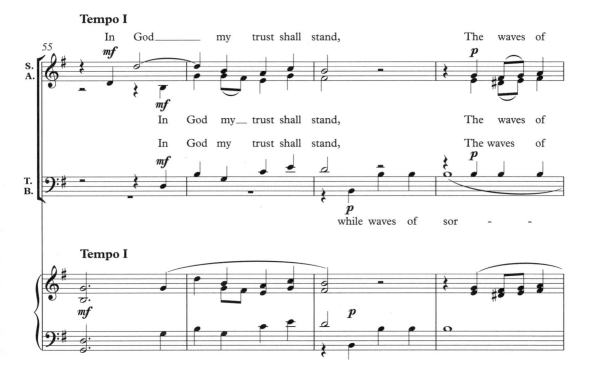

Commissioned by the University of Nebraska–Lincoln's
Glenn Korff School of Music
for the George Walker Festival, 5 April 2022

We are the music makers

Arthur O'Shaughnessy
(1844 –81)

REGINAL WRIGHT

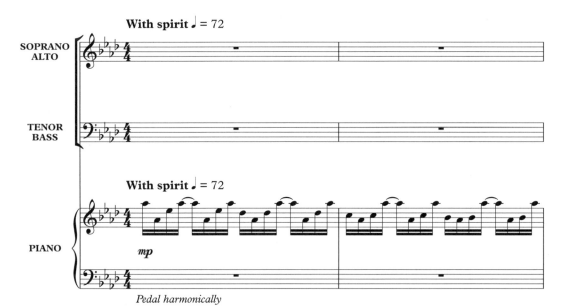

Also available in a version for SSA and piano (ISBN 978–0–19–356417–6).

Duration: 2 mins

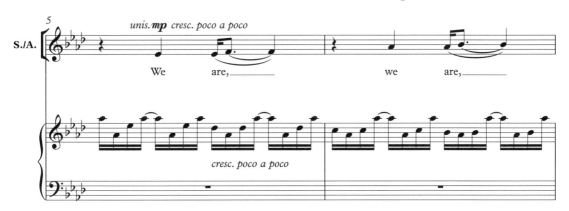

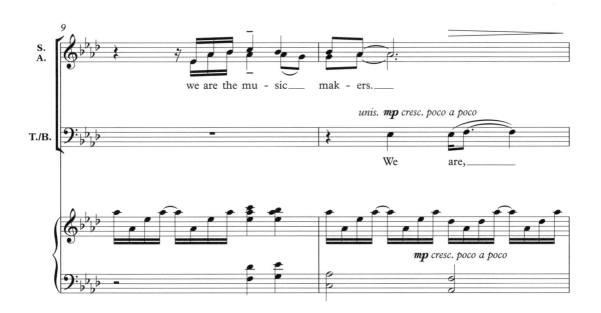

* Small notes denote optional *divisi*.

we are the mu - sic mak - ers, ____ the ____

we are the mu - sic mak - ers, ____ the ____

dream - ers, ____ we are the dream - ers ____ of ____

dream - ers, ____ we are the dream - ers ____ of

dreams.

dreams.

COMMENTARY

Notes

A shorthand system to identify the variants found in the sources is employed as follows: bar number (Arabic), voice (S1, S2, A1, A2, *etc.*), and symbol number in the bar (Roman). For example, in Coleman *The 100th Psalm*, 51 B *i* refers to bar/measure 51, Bass, first note of the bar.

No source has been listed when the work is by a living composer and has not been published prior to this anthology.

1. Adams: *Hosanna to the Son of David*

H. Leslie Adams (b. 1932) is a celebrated composer of instrumental and vocal works. Several research projects on his music have focused on his significant output of solo vocal music. Two notable song cycles, *Nightsongs* and *Five Millay Songs*, express a wide range of emotions, including desperation, longing, love, and joy, while his magnum opus, *Blake*, is an opera/musical drama about losing and finding love in the Antebellum South. Adams earned degrees from Oberlin College (Conservatory of Music), Long Beach State University, and The Ohio State University and taught at and conducted the choir of the University of Kansas before becoming a freelance composer. He has received the 'Life Achievement Award' of the Cleveland Arts Prize from his birth city. Adapted from the Gospels of St Matthew and St Mark, *Hosanna to the Son of David* is a jubilant anthem replete with primarily conjunct melodies and louder dynamics announcing the arrival of the Messiah.

Source: First edition (Walton Music Corp., 1976).

2. Boykin: *Music of Life*

Composer, conductor, and pianist Brittney Boykin (B. E. Boykin) (b. 1989) first pursued her interest in composition during her time at Spelman College, attending classes that inspired and challenged her musical imagination. After graduating with a BA in Music, Boykin continued choral composition and arrangement while attending Westminster Choir College of Rider University in Princeton, New Jersey, graduating with a MMus in Sacred Music and receiving the R & R Young Composition Prize. She obtained her PhD from Georgia State University with an emphasis in Music Education. Among her professional endeavours, Boykin has been featured as the conductor/composer-in-residence for the 2017 Harry T. Burleigh Commemorative Spiritual Festival at Tennessee State University. She is an Assistant Professor of Music at the Georgia Institute of Technology in addition to her active commission and conducting schedule. *Music of Life* is an ethereal setting of a poem by George Parsons Lathrop (1851–98) that describes how music underpins all earthly life. The pulsating piano part effervesces with the life and music in 'all growing things'.

3. Brown: *O praise the Lord*

As an alumnus of Morehouse College in Atlanta, Georgia, Uzee Brown, Jr. (b. 1950) serves his alma mater as Professor of Music and Chair of the Division of Creative and Performing Arts. He grew up in the Piedmont region of South Carolina in a small town called Cowpens. While he keeps his heritage alive by utilizing idiomatic music from his childhood, his original works display a varied approach to text that can be traced back to his teachers and mentors, who include Wendell P. Whalum, T. J. Anderson, and Willis Patterson. Brown earned graduate degrees at Bowling Green State University and Michigan State University. His compositions have been performed at the 1996 Centennial Olympics, Morehouse College ceremonies and celebrations, and in the 1988 film *School Daze*. His notable positions include co-founder and chairman of the Board of Directors of Onyx Opera Atlanta and president of the National Association of Negro Musicians, Inc. Brown is also a celebrated singer and a researcher, focusing on spirituals and art songs by Black composers. *O praise the Lord* is a celebratory anthem with a dazzling organ part. The homophonic exclamations resound the communal praise of Psalm 117.

4. Burton: *A Prayer*

Ken Burton (b. 1970) is a musician whose philosophy of 'it's all equal' manifests in his varied roles, which include conductor, composer, presenter, adjudicator, and producer. His upbringing as the last child of ten in a West Indian Christian family saw his musical relationship develop through service music and devotions. For two decades, Burton has served as the conductor of the London Adventist Chorale, a choir comprised of members of various Seventh-day Adventist Churches. Additionally, his television work includes *Songs of Praise*, *Prom at the Palace*, and *Soul Noel*, and he is credited as choirmaster for the blockbuster film *Black Panther*. As a composer, Burton's unique musical language at times combines his classical and gospel backgrounds. He has received commissions from The Choir of St John's College, Cambridge, the Aldeburgh Music Festival, and VOCES8. *A Prayer* was written for the debut concert of the Jason Max Ferdinand Singers in 2021. The chromatic lines move effortlessly to highlight the simple, strophic text by Paul Laurence Dunbar (1872–1906). Spirituals and jazz also permeate each stanza with syncopations and extended harmonies.

Source: manuscript edition in possession of the editor from the debut performance.

5. Coleman: *The 100th Psalm*

A native of Detroit, Michigan, Charles D. Coleman (1929–91) graduated from Wayne State University in 1954. He worked at various Detroit public schools and with several churches. Very little is written about Coleman. His works are held in the Archives of African American Music and Culture at Indiana University, Bloomington, and two-thirds of these are in manuscript form. Most of his music was published by Northwestern School of Music Press. While his choral writing is largely homophonic, his polyphonic passages often feature imitation and sustained pitches for contrast. *The 100th Psalm* in modified ternary form captures the joy and excitement of the familiar psalm. Unlike in some of his other anthems, the soprano range is limited to pitches on the stave, without extensions into the extremes. The organ part features a fanfare-like motif that effectively complements the text.

Source: Charles Coleman Papers, 1929–1991; SC 9: Box 1/3; Archives of African American Music and Culture, Indiana University, Bloomington. *Variants*: changed all text to match KJV / removed unnecessary divisi doubled in soprano or alto / eliminated solo phrase slurs / added missing dots to correct rhythms / 14–16 & 18–20: applied accidentals in a different manuscript ink colour and altered choir rhythm to avoid harsh dissonance / 40 Solo: aligned rhythm with organ like previous measures / 51 B *i*: confirmation that Bass rhythm in manuscript is different from SAT / 53 organ *iv*: altered last beat to match D.S. / 61 organ: added missing beams.

6. Butler: *Dona nobis pacem*

Mark Butler (b. 1965) is an acclaimed composer and conductor with degrees from Florida A&M University (FAMU), Florida State University, and The American Conservatory of Music. As Director of Choral Activities and Studies at FAMU, he has conducted several major choral–orchestral works and made history in 2021 when the FAMU Concert Choir became the first choir to perform the Black American national anthem, *Lift Every Voice and Sing*, at the National Football League Kickoff game in Tampa, Florida. His arrangement of *Glory Hallelujah to the New Born King* was performed by the Boys and Girls Choir of Harlem on *Good Morning America*. While he is skilled at creating fiery arrangements of Negro spirituals, his original works for choir give equal attention to text and affect. *Dona nobis pacem* is a sensitive setting combining two lines of traditional Latin text about peace. The lush harmonies and flowing lines create a sense of yearning for peace for all people. The work was composed in 2010 and may be performed in the alternative key of B major.

Translation: Grant us peace. And on earth, peace to men of good will.

7. Carter: *Psalm 131*

Nathan Carter (1936–2004) was born in Selma, Alabama, and began taking piano lessons as early as the age of five. He graduated from Hampton Institute (now University) and earned degrees from The Juilliard School and the Peabody Institute of The Johns Hopkins University. Under Carter's thirty-plus years of leadership, the Morgan State University Choir developed national and international recognition, with notable performances at the Kennedy Center with the National Symphony Orchestra, at Carnegie Hall's 100th anniversary tribute to Marian Anderson in 1997, and in South Africa at the invitation of Archbishop Desmond Tutu. Students from his choir have gone on to celebrated careers as soloists, choristers, and conductors. As a champion of the music of Black composers, Carter prepared the chorus for and conducted several recordings of large-scale choral–orchestral works by composers such as Adolphus Hailstork, José Maurício Nunes Garcia, William Grant Still, and George Walker. As a composer, he is best known for the grandeur of his many hymn arrangements. *Psalm 131* is a prelude and fugue beginning with a homophonic treatment of the first two verses. The final verse in the minor mode returns the work to its opening compound duple metre, with flowing rhythmic movement throughout.

Source: First edition (GIA Publications Inc., 2005). *Variant*: 43 B1 *vi*: added optional alternative note for performability.

8. Coleridge-Taylor: *By the lone seashore*

Born to an African father and an English mother, Samuel Coleridge-Taylor (1875–1912) was named after the English poet Samuel Taylor Coleridge. He studied violin at the Royal College of Music before switching to composition. Some of his early success resulted from the premiere of his *Ballade in A Minor* (Op. 33) at the Three Choirs Festival in Gloucester in 1898, where he was recommended by Edward Elgar (1857–1934). Shortly thereafter, the premiere of *Hiawatha's Wedding Feast*, conducted by his teacher Charles Villiers Stanford (1852–1924), was an immediate hit among audiences, solidifying his position among the other great composers of his short life. He was later commissioned to compose two additional cantatas, also with texts by Henry Wadsworth Longfellow (1807–82), that serve as a trilogy titled *The Song of Hiawatha* (Op. 30). His admiration of Longfellow's poetry can be seen in the naming of his son, Hiawatha. His daughter, Avril, became a composer and conductor. His American success resulted in three American tours and the formation of the Samuel Coleridge-Taylor Choral Society of Washington, DC, a group of 200 Black singers in the early twentieth century formed to perform his music. He later dedicated *Three Choral Ballads* (Op. 54) to the organization. Aside from his *24 Negro Melodies* (Op. 59(1)) for piano, little of his music displays any influence of Black music idioms. *By the lone seashore* is an unaccompanied part-song set at a slow tempo to reflect mourning and sadness. The plethora of semitones and lilting triple metre imitate the rocking of the waves along the shore.

Source: First edition (Novello and Company, 1901, published in *The Musical Times and Singing Class Circular*, vol. 24, no. 699 (May 1, 1901)). *Variant*: 90 ATB *i*: note-length shortened to match Sopranos.

9. Coleridge-Taylor: *The Lord is my strength*

The Lord is my strength is a short Easter anthem combining text from Psalm 118—for the first two sections in B♭ and E♭—and two hymn texts from *Hymns Ancient and Modern* translated by John Mason Neale (1818–66) for the concluding chorale. The three contrasting sections feature full harmonies with little imitation, divided unison melodies, and homophonic phrases with final fermatas respectively.

Source: First edition (Novello, Ewer and Co., 1892). *Variants*: registrations are editorial except bar/measure 61 / 84: 'Chorale' tempo is editorial.

10. Dett: *Son of Mary*

R. Nathaniel Dett (1882–1943) was a Canadian-born composer who lived most of his life in the United States. He was the first Black graduate of Oberlin College, where he majored in piano and composition. In addition to his master's degree at the Eastman School of Music, he studied at Harvard University and at the American Conservatory at Fontainebleau with Nadia Boulanger. His fame as a composer came through his choral works, despite being an accomplished pianist with six piano suites and other works for solo voice and instruments to his name. Early success came after the publication of *Listen to the Lambs* (1914), which carried the description 'a religious characteristic in the form of an anthem' and combined his original setting of Isaiah 40:11 with the eponymous spiritual. This was one of his early efforts at using Black folk music to create anthems, motets, and oratorios with the aim of preserving the music and demonstrating its value beyond the traditional folk-song arrangement. In 1920, he won the Francis Boott Prize at Harvard University for his motet *Don't Be Weary, Traveler*, which also combines a spiritual and a Biblical text. As an educator, Dett started Hampton Institute's music department and elevated the reputation of their choir. *Son of Mary* is a jubilant motet 'based on a traditional Negro melody' from Dett's personal collection and sets a text by Henry Hart Milman (1791–1868). The unknown pentatonic melody is reminiscent of a spiritual, and Dett's counterpoint adds rhythmic vitality throughout the final verse's fugato with its own syncopated rhythms.

Source: First edition (John Church Company, 1926). *Variants*: 18 S & B: Dett used 'feeble' not 'throbbing' as written in *The Hymnal* (published by the Authority of the General Assembly of the Presbyterian Church in the USA, 1895) / 56: changed 'ben ritmo sed poco allargamente' to 'Ben ritmico e largamente' / 64–70: Dett used 'When our eyes grow dim in death, When we heave the parting breath, When our final doom is near,' not 'When the solemn death-bell tolls For our own departing souls, When our solemn doom is near' / 83: composer's original 'human' changed to 'mortal' in line with Henry Hart Milman's text. This is the only time that 'human' is used instead of 'mortal'.

11. Furman: *Four Little Foxes*

James Furman (1937–89) was born in Louisville, Kentucky, and earned his bachelor's and master's degrees at the University of Louisville. After working at Louisville's Church of Our Merciful Saviour, teaching in the public school system, and serving in the military, his final appointment was at Western Connecticut State University where he worked until he died. His compositional output includes works in the classical and gospel genres. Most choral musicians know him for the exuberant unaccompanied work *Hehlehlooyuh* (*A Joyful Expression*). His oratorio *I Have a Dream*—a commission from the Greenwich Choral Society (Danbury, Connecticut) in commemoration of their 45th anniversary—was dedicated to the memory of Martin Luther King, Jr. *Four Little Foxes* is a contrasting set of four miniatures with text by Lew Sarett (1888–1954). Furman set the poem's four stanzas separately, using minimal imitation with clusters and extended harmonies. Composed in 1963, the unaccompanied miniatures are rich in word painting and present an exciting challenge for choirs.

Sources: First edition (Oxford University Press, 1971); The James Furman Collection, Center for Black Music Research Collection, Columbia College Chicago, Chicago, Illinois, Box 5. *Variants*: all variants added from original manuscript. 1. Speak Gently – added 'moving' to opening tempo indication / 1 SATB: changed 'poco' to '*mp*' / 3 Alto *iv*: E changed to G. 2. Walk Softly – 11: added 'with stability'. 3. Go Lightly – changed tempo to 76 / 13 S: added hairpin / 13 A & B: changed hairpins to match the manuscript.

12. Garcia: *Ave maris stella*, CPM 21

José Maurício Nunes Garcia (1767–1830) was born, lived, and died in Rio de Janeiro. After the death of his father, his mother and aunt recognized his musical abilities and enrolled him in music classes. Garcia is one of the most important and revered musical figures of the early nineteenth century in Brazil. He was ordained as a priest in 1792 and appointed *mestre de capela* of Rio de Janeiro Cathedral in 1798. Garcia's success rests on several important musical moments. In 1808, he was appointed *mestre de capela* of the royal chapel by Dom João VI of Portugal—the most important musical position in the kingdom. His 1817 opera *Le due gemelle* was the first opera composed and premiered in Brazil. Garcia's musical output includes at least 237 compositions, with sacred music for the Catholic church abounding. Of his four requiems and nineteen masses, the requiem of 1816 (CPM 186) and *Mass of St Cecilia* of 1826 (CPM 113) are the pinnacle of his career as a composer. Both were written toward the end of his life, with the latter being the final work he composed. Garcia's music is akin to the Viennese School of his European Classical contemporaries. Garcia composed *Ave maris stella* for mixed choir with a small instrumental ensemble of flutes, horns, strings, and organ, presented here in an orchestral reduction by Alec Schumacker. This short hymn is primarily homophonic, with joyful dynamic contrasts in adoration and praise of the Virgin Mary.

Translation: Hail, star of the sea, nurturing Mother of God, and ever Virgin, happy gate of Heaven. *Source*: Acervo Cleofe Person de Mattos, 65.21.01, reproduction. *Variant*: copyist's 'D.C.' marking shown as a repeat sign.

13. Garcia: *Alleluia, angelus Domini, CPM 140*

Alleluia, angelus Domini is a Christmas gradual, with text from the second chapter of the book of Matthew depicting the moment that the angel tells Joseph to take his family to Egypt. The original instrumentation is flute, two horns, strings, and organ, and Alec Schumacker has prepared an orchestral reduction for piano for this collection.

Translation: Alleluia. The angel of the Lord appeared in a dream to Joseph and said, 'Get up and take the boy and his mother and flee into Egypt.' Alleluia. *Sources*: Acervo da coleção Bento das Mercês e adquirido pelo Governo da República e doado ao INM, em fins de 1897. *Variant* (in consultation with co-editor, Alec Schumacker): 4 piano: changed bass rhythm to match bar/measure 2.

14. Garrett: *My heart be brave*

Marques L. A. Garrett is an established conductor, educator, and composer whose works have been performed to acclaim by high school all-state, collegiate, and professional choirs, including Seraphic Fire and the Aeolians of Oakwood University. Awarded a PhD in Music Education (Choral Conducting) from Florida State University, Dr Garrett is an Assistant Professor of Music in Choral Activities at the University of Nebraska–Lincoln. He also serves as artistic director and conductor of the Omaha Symphonic Chorus and as founding artistic director and conductor of the Nebraska Festival Singers. *My heart be brave* was the result of a request from Dr Anthony Trecek-King for a work that aligned with the social justice theme of his concerts with Seraphic Fire. The first and last lines of the poem by James Weldon Johnson (1871–1938) immediately stood out: in the midst of discrimination, our heart—the core of our being—must lead us into rightful change. And as we continue doing right, the principles of honesty, love, and justice will give us the power to strive for what is due to all of humanity.

15. Geter: *The Gift to Sing*

Damien Geter (b. 1980) is a composer and vocalist based in Chicago, Illinois. As a bass-baritone, he has sung with the Metropolitan Opera and the Seattle Opera, and he has served as Artistic Advisor and interim Music Director for Portland Opera. He has written for choir, orchestra, opera, solo voice, organ, and chamber ensembles, with commissions from Washington National Opera and the University of Michigan. Larger works such as *An African American Requiem* (commissioned by Resonance Ensemble) and *Cantata for a More Hopeful Tomorrow* (commissioned by The Washington Chorus) represent his desire to use music for social justice. *The Gift to Sing* is an unaccompanied part-song for mixed choir with text by James Weldon Johnson. (One of Johnson's most famous texts, 'Lift Every Voice and Sing', was set to music by

his brother J. Rosamond Johnson (1873–1954) and nicknamed the Negro National Anthem.) Geter paints the text 'I pierce the darkness with a note' with sustained pitches that depict the piercing. The overall prevailing triple metre gives momentum to the lilting melodies that weave through the voices.

16. Hailstork: *God be merciful*

Adolphus Hailstork (b. 1941) is one of the most prolific American composers of his generation. He studied at Howard University, Manhattan School of Music, the American Conservatory at Fontainebleau, and Michigan State University, earning degrees in theory and composition. He taught and was composer-in-residence at Norfolk State University and is Professor Emeritus at Old Dominion University in Norfolk, Virginia. Among many high-profile performances of his music was the inclusion of the wind-band arrangement of his *Fanfare on 'Amazing Grace'* at the inauguration of the US President Joe Biden in 2021. While his output ranges from compositions for solo piano and voice to orchestral works and opera, choral music is his favourite medium, and his early choral influences come from singing at an Episcopalian cathedral as a young child. In 1999, he was awarded the Raymond W. Brock Memorial Commission by the American Choral Directors Association, for which he wrote *The God of Glory Thunders*. *God be merciful* is a predominantly homophonic setting of the first three-and-a-half verses of Psalm 67 in the King James translation. This reverential prayer emphasizes 'God' with multiple sustained pitches.

17. Harris, C. H.: *Bring me all your dreams*

Christopher H. Harris (b. 1985) earned degrees from Florida State University, Ithaca College, and Texas Southern University. He has worked as a public-school teacher in Houston, Texas, and as Director of Choral Activities at Arkansas Tech University. Aside from his teaching responsibilities, his conducting credits include serving as the founder of the Houston Master Singers and assistant director for the Houston Ebony Opera Guild. His choirs have sung at several state and regional conferences of professional organizations. Harris's music has been performed by several high-profile professional and all-state choirs and he receives regular commissions from choirs of various abilities. He frequently collaborates with lyricist Devondra Banks. A gentle setting of familiar words by Langston Hughes (1902–67), *Bring me all your dreams* is a quintessential example of Harris's effective homophonic writing and employment of lush harmonies.

18. Harris, R. A.: *April Rain Song*

Robert A. Harris (b. 1938) is Professor Emeritus at Northwestern University's Bienen School of Music and served as Professor of Conducting and Director of Choral Organisations from 1977 to 2012. He has been a visiting professor at Wayne State University, the University of Texas at Austin, and the University of South Africa in Pretoria, and he has served as director of music and choirmaster at the Winnetka Congregational Church in Illinois. Harris has received several awards, including an Alumni Arts Achievement Award in Music from Wayne State University and a Northwestern University Alumni Association Excellence in Teaching Award. Numerous schools, churches, and musical organizations have commissioned him for choral music, and he has been widely published. *April Rain Song* is an atmospheric *a cappella* setting where Langston Hughes's evocative text and Harris's expressive vocal lines combine to encapsulate the familiarity of rain.

19. Harris, R. A.: *Oh, how can I keep from singing?*
Setting the text of the traditional folk hymn of the same name, *Oh, how can I keep from singing?* combines an original melody with uniquely independent vocal lines in all parts. The slow tempo allows the frequent metre shifts to be unobtrusive.

Source: First edition (Oxford University Press, 1988).

20. Hurd: *Ecce sacerdos magnus*
David Hurd (b. 1950) is an educator, composer, and organist. He studied at The Juilliard School, Oberlin College, and the University of North Carolina at Chapel Hill, and he has taught at Duke University, The General Theological Seminary, Manhattan School of Music, Westminster Choir College, and Yale University. Hurd's work as a church organist and on stage has garnered numerous awards. In 1977, he won first prize in both organ performance and improvisation from the International Congress of Organists and in 2010 received The American Guild of Organists' Distinguished Composer Award. Hurd's name is synonymous with church music as his small- and large-scale vocal and organ works are used in services throughout the United States, with several of his hymns and other service music published in various hymnals. As the composer writes, *Ecce sacerdos magnus* 'was composed in 1975 for the liturgical greeting of the Right Reverend Paul Moore, Bishop of New York, at an interparish festival service at the Chapel of the Intercession (Trinity Parish), New York City. It is entirely based upon the mode 8 plainsong responsory for the reception of a bishop as found in the *Liber Usualis*', and it begins with parallel fifths in the organ that shift to doubled vocal lines. Hurd's quintessential style is reminiscent of modal melodies. The grandeur of dynamics and fullness of this accompanied motet complement the celebratory text describing the blessings of the priest.

Translation: Behold the high priest, who in his days pleased God. Therefore, by an oath, the Lord made him increase among his people. He gave him the blessing of all nations and confirmed his covenant upon his head. Glory be to the Father, and to the Son, and to the Holy Spirit.

21. Kay: *As Joseph was a-walking*
Ulysses Kay (1917–95) studied piano, violin, and saxophone at the University of Arizona, the Eastman School of Music, Yale University, and Columbia University. He was a fellow at the Berkshire Music Center (now Tanglewood) and was awarded a Fulbright scholarship, an Alice M. Ditson Fellowship, and a Julius Rosenwald Fellowship. He worked as an editor at Broadcast Music, Inc., during the day and at night composed and taught at Lehman College of the City University of New York. Kay is known for his neoclassical style. Tonality generally frames his music while non-functional chromaticism provides additional colours. His oeuvre comprises small choral works, chamber music, film and television scores, large orchestral works, and several operas. *As Joseph was a-walking* began as a three-part unaccompanied work in 1943 'to the Eastman School Chorus' and was later altered and expanded to include a fourth vocal line. This Christmas piece demonstrates hallmarks of Kay's style such as modal harmonies, imitation, and the occasional use of word painting.

Source: Ulysses Kay papers, 1938–1995; Series II: Music by Kay, 1939–1991, Box 6 Folder 30; Holograph of four-part version, circa, 1955; Rare Book & Manuscript Library, Columbia University Libraries.

22. Kay: *How stands the glass around?*
How stands the glass around? was written in 1954 in the style of a madrigal, at the request of David Randolph for his five-member group, the David Randolph Singers, formed in 1943. Their album *Lament for April 15 and Other Modern American Madrigals* contains both madrigals that Kay wrote for the group. Kay explored the militaristic text, by British Army officer James Wolfe (1727–59), through competing rhythms to intimate a battle. Evident throughout the work is Kay's penchant for idiomatic vocal writing and the use of imitation.

Source: First edition (Associated Music Publishers, Inc., 1956).

23. King: *Psalm 57*
Betty Jackson King (1928–94) is best known for her choral and solo vocal works. Several of her choral works are sacred in nature, reflecting her upbringing: her father was a pastor and part of the reason for her deep religious faith. Although she grew up in Chicago, her family's time in Mississippi brought about the influence of spirituals—particularly those heard at church—and she later arranged spirituals for various choral scorings. King earned a Bachelor of Arts degree in piano and a master's degree in composition from the Chicago Musical College of Roosevelt University. In her professional life, she formed and served as the conductor of The Betty Jackson King Artists, who performed in the Chicago area. She later served as a president of the National Association of Negro Musicians, Inc. *Psalm 57* was published in 1972 and is dedicated to the Brazeal Dennard Chorale, a Detroit-based choir that championed the music of Black composers. An unaccompanied setting that contrasts moments of reflection with declamatory exultation, the piece uses portions of four verses of Psalm 57 in the

King James translation.

Source: First edition (Jacksonian Press, Inc., 1972). *Variants*: 58: added 'a tempo' / 99: reduction updated to match choir pitches.

24. Lusitano: *Emendemus in melius*

Vicente Lusitano (*c*.1520–*c*.1561) was a Portuguese theorist and composer. (It is plausible that Lusitano may not be his family name as it is sometimes seen as a nickname for Portugal/Portuguese.) Aside from a 1982 article by Robert Stevenson and brief encyclopaedia entries, Lusitano's name existed in relative obscurity for centuries. One possible reason might be the debate between Lusitano and fellow theorist and composer Nicola Vicentino (1511–*c*.1576) on whether a *Regina caeli* by an unnamed composer was purely diatonic or not. Although Lusitano was victorious, Vicentino's published recollection of the debate likely stained Lusitano's reputation. After the slander, Lusitano left Portugal and moved to Germany, where he converted to Protestantism. Lusitano is considered the first composer of African descent to have had music published, and his compositions influenced other composers, including Carlo Gesualdo. Moreover, one of Vicentino's madrigals appears to quote Lusitano's highly chromatic motet *Heu me, Domine*, which had already been published. Originally, *Emendemus in melius* was a two-part motet like his famous *Regina caeli*. The text is the responsory for Ash Wednesday/the First Sunday of Lent and the scoring of this edition has been given as SAATB. *Musica ficta* above pitches are suggestions for these pitches to be altered, as performers during this time period would have done naturally; they are at the discretion of the performers and conductors. The editorial practice section on page viii of this anthology provides more information about the preparation of this edition.

Translation: Let us amend for the better in those things in which we have sinned through ignorance; lest suddenly overtaken by the day of death, we seek space for repentance, and be not able to find it. Hear, O Lord, and have mercy: for we have sinned against you. *Source*: Liber primus epigramatum (1555): Prima pars: raised a minor third / rhythms halved; Supranus – Soprano; Quinta – Alto 1; Altus – Alto 2; Tenor – Tenor; Bassus – Bass. *Variants*: 51 S *ii*: substituted 'qui' for 'ii' in Supranus.

25. Margetson: *A few more years shall roll*

Edward Margetson (1891–1962) was born in St Kitts, British West Indies, to musical parents. He immigrated to the United States in 1919 and began serving as organist and choirmaster of the Church of the Crucifixion in New York City a year later. He went on to create the Schubert Music Society of New York as an artistic outlet for the Black population. Margetson held a celebrated tenure at Columbia University, and his archives are located in Columbia's Rare Book & Manuscript Library. As well as writing music for choir and solo voice, he was also a member of the American Guild of Organists. Until recently, the only score of his numerous choral pieces still available in print was a reissue of *He stooped to bless*. *A few more years shall roll* sets a hymn by Horatius Bonar (1808–89) that was written for his congregation to use on New Year's Day. It is like *He stooped to bless* in its use of imitative motifs at the end of large sections and tonal writing that is coupled with facile modulations.

Source: Edward H. Margetson Music Manuscripts, 1917–1962; Series IV: Sacred Choruses (mixed voices), Box 1 Folder 4; Rare Book & Manuscript Library, Columbia University Libraries.

26. Moore, D. R.: *In Celebration*

Dorothy Rudd Moore (1940–2022) is considered a leading figure among her generation of African American composers. She was always interested in music and received support from her parents to pursue music as a career. She studied with Dean Warner Lawson, Thomas Kerr, and Mark Fax at Howard University before graduating in 1963. After studies with Nadia Boulanger and Chou Wen-Chung, she co-founded the Society of Black Composers. As a composer of choral, solo vocal, and chamber works—plus extended cycles and the opera *Frederick Douglass*, for which she also wrote the libretto—her music has been recorded and performed around the world. *In Celebration* was composed in 1977 and combines 'Words like Freedom' by Langston Hughes with excerpts from three of his other poems. Moore's expansive harmonic language enables the texts to combine seamlessly. The piece includes significant solos for soprano and baritone. *Source*: First edition (American Composers Alliance (BMI), 2016). *Variants*: 82 T *iii*: adjusted C octave for cross voicing / 83 T *i*: adjusted D♭ octave.

27. Moore, U. S.: *I, too*

Undine Smith Moore (1904–89) is often referred to as the 'Dean of Black Women Composers' due to her famed career and influence on many Black composers of the twentieth and twenty-first centuries. She held a significant teaching tenure at Virginia State College (now University) in Petersburg, Virginia. The celebrated and frequent performances of her spiritual arrangements have cemented her catalogue in American choral libraries. She was, however, equally versed in writing original music and is particularly esteemed for her choral music. Her magnum opus is the extended work *Scenes from the Life of a Martyr* for choir, soloists, and orchestra, written about Dr Martin Luther King, Jr. Langston Hughes was a frequent source of inspiration, with Moore setting his poems in works such as *Mother to Son*, *Tambourines to Glory*, and *When Susanna Jones Wears Red*. As evidenced in *I, too*, which also uses text by Langston Hughes, her original music is highly sensitive to the text, with textual structure determining the musical structure—each new set of text is given a distinct musical idea that seldom returns. She completed at least two versions of this choral art song, with changes in the middle sections.

Source: manuscript facsimile in editor's possession as gifted by composer's former colleague

Carl G. Harris, Jr.—this is one of two versions of a manuscript, both without a date. *Variants*: 33: 'a tempo' changed to 'Tempo I' / 35: original 'virile, manly tone' replaced with 'strong tone' / 45: alternative version is in 3/4 with a series of parallel fourths in voices and piano / 72: added 'allargando e marcato' from alternative version.

28. McLin: *See what love*
An author, composer, teacher, and ordained minister, Lena J. McLin (b. 1928) was born in Atlanta, Georgia. When she first moved to Chicago, she lived with her uncle, Thomas A. Dorsey, known as the father of gospel music. She earned degrees at Spelman College and the American Conservatory of Music, completing further studies at Roosevelt University and Chicago State University. Alongside her husband, Nathanael McLin, she founded the McLin Opera Company in the mid-1950s, and she also served as a minister of music at Trinity Congregational Church in Chicago. McLin had an influential teaching career, with several of her former students enjoying celebrated careers in varied genres of music including opera, jazz, and R&B. McLin's vast output includes masses, operas, anthems, and popular songs, in addition to works for solo voice and choir where she explores styles such as gospel, jazz, and rock. Her experience in the Black church and with gospel music and spirituals influences some, but not all, of her music. Her larger works include *Free at Last: A Portrait of Martin Luther King, Jr.* and *Gwendolyn Brooks: A Musical Portrait*. *See what love* is a beautifully simple unaccompanied anthem that sets two verses from the third chapter of 1 John. The piece is mostly homophonic, with a contrasting moment of imitation.
Source: First edition (General Words and Music Co., 1982). *Variant*: clarified repeats.

29. Perry: *Song of our Savior*
Julia Perry (1924–79) was born in Lexington, Kentucky, and studied voice, piano, and composition at Westminster Choir College, with graduate study at the Berkshire Music Center (now Tanglewood) and The Juilliard School. Later, she taught at Florida A&M College (now University) and Atlanta University. She received awards from the National Institute of Arts and Letters and the National Association of Negro Musicians, Inc., and in 1952 she won the Boulanger Grand Prix for her Violin Sonata. After a stroke, Perry taught herself to write with her left hand in order to continue composing. While her early works make references to her African American heritage, her style centres around the traditional classical music she learned from her studies in the United States and in Europe—where she studied after winning two Guggenheim Fellowships—under Luigi Dallapiccola and Nadia Boulanger. She composed twelve symphonies, three operas, and other smaller works. *Song of our Savior* was dedicated to the Hampton Institute Choir and contains passages for a soprano soloist. This unaccompanied anthem with words by Perry features two prominent melodic ostinatos that switch between

all the voice parts. The text describes the life of Jesus as Mary and Joseph reflect on many important events from the Bible.
Source: First edition (Galaxy Music Corporation, 1953).

30. Price: *Resignation*
Florence Price (1887–1953) was born in Little Rock, Arkansas, and studied piano from an early age. She earned two diplomas at the New England Conservatory in Boston and taught at Shorter College and Clark Atlanta University. Price was a pioneer for Black women in composition, and her compositions include symphonies, concertos, art songs, chamber music, choral works, and numerous works for solo piano. Despite facing barriers of racism and sexism in her professional career, she went on to be the first Black woman to have a symphony performed by a major American orchestra, in 1933. She also won prizes for her Symphony in E Minor, Piano Sonata, and song *Sea Ghost*. After the discovery of a substantial collection of Price's manuscripts in 2009, there has been a renewed interest in her music, which had mostly sat unperformed by mainstream musicians. While spiritual arrangements did not dominate her output, Price was influenced by them in her original works, including *Resignation*, which features a repeated, folk-like, pentatonic melody. Price wrote both words and music for *Resignation*, which she composed in versions for solo voice and piano and for unaccompanied mixed voices. The date of composition is not known.
Source: First edition (G. Schirmer, Inc., 2020).

31. Simon: *Sanctus*
Prior to his faculty position at Georgetown University, Carlos Simon (b. 1986) taught at Spelman College and his alma mater Morehouse College, both in his native city of Atlanta, Georgia. He later earned degrees from Georgia State University and the University of Michigan. Even in this early stage of his compositional career, he was one of the recipients of the 2021 Sphinx Medal of Excellence, the highest honour awarded by the Sphinx Organization, recognizing extraordinary classical Black and Latinx musicians. He also received the 2016 Underwood Emerging Composer Commission from the American Composers Orchestra and the Presser Award from the Presser Foundation in 2015. Simon has been commissioned by the New York Philharmonic, LA Opera, Morehouse College, and the American Composers Orchestra, among others. In 2021, he was appointed as a composer-in-residence at the Kennedy Center, writing music for the National Symphony Orchestra and Washington National Opera. Simon's upbringing in a Black church rooted in gospel music weaves its way into several of his works. The titles of some of his instrumental pieces reflect his cultural heritage, namely *Amen!*, *Plagues of Egypt*, *Portrait of a Queen*, *Sweet Chariot*, and *Where two or three are gathered*. As evidenced in his works, his musical influences are not limited to classical music. *Sanctus* for mixed choir and piano is one of Simon's earliest works.

The simple piece features seamless swift harmonic shifts and ethereal whispered text at the opening.

Translation: Holy, holy, holy, Lord, God of Sabaoth. Heaven and earth are full of your glory. Hosanna in the highest. *Source*: First edition (GIA Publications, Inc., 2008).

32. Robles: *Magnificat*

Zanaida Stewart Robles (b. 1979) is an award-winning composer, conductor, vocalist, clinician, and adjudicator who holds a Doctor of Musical Arts degree from the USC Thornton School of Music. She was appointed director of music at Neighborhood Unitarian Universalist Church in Pasadena, California, in 2018, and has been commissioned to compose for choirs across the United States including Tonality and the Southern Tier Singers' Collective. She is a fierce supporter of the diversification of choral repertoire and improving the understanding of inclusion in music education and performance. *Magnificat* is a challenging but rewarding setting of the familiar text in its English translation, with occasional Latin interjections, and features rapid twists and turns in the interweaving melodies. It is a movement from the complete work *Magnificat and Nunc Dimittis*. A version of this work with piano and organ accompaniment—a combination that reflects the tradition of the Black American church in which the composer grew up, where both instruments were used simultaneously for almost all service music—is also available.

33. Weston: *Rivers of Living Water*

Trevor Weston (b. 1967) received his BA in music and history from Tufts University and continued his studies at the University of California, Berkeley, where he earned his MA and PhD in Music Composition. He was appointed Music Department chair at Drew University in 2009 and as an Instructor on the Music Advancement Program at The Juilliard School in 2019. His honours include the Arts and Letters Award in Music and a Goddard Lieberson Fellowship from the American Academy of Arts and Letters, the George Ladd Prix de Paris from the University of California, Berkeley, and residencies from the Virginia Center for the Creative Arts and MacDowell. Deeply inspired by music that mesmerises and entrances its listeners by creating a sense of suspended reality, Weston creates music that is transformative—through which both performer and audience can retreat from the mundane to reflect more profoundly on existence. *Rivers of Living Water* is an accessible setting of verses from John 7 that depicts the 'rivers of living water' and contrasting 'parched land' in episodic form. An independent, atmospheric organ part underpins long, interweaving vocal lines, all of which sit within a comfortable vocal range.

34. Work: *The sun himself shall fade*

John Wesley Work III (1901–67) was from a musical family. His father was a noted ethnomusicologist and among the first to collect Negro spirituals and other Black folk music. Being from Tennessee and having familial connections to Fisk University, he naturally attended the school before continuing at Yale to earn a bachelor's degree. Among his other educational pursuits, he studied composition in New York before returning to Nashville to serve as chairman of the Fisk Department of Music and director of the Fisk Jubilee Singers. While Work's career was closely tied to spirituals as a likely result of his family's musical heritage, he also composed sacred and secular music for choirs and solo voice. His cantata *The Singers* won first prize in the 1946 competition by the Federation of American Composers. While *The sun himself shall fade* is firmly rooted in the classical tradition, the anthem features call and response between the sopranos and the rest of the choir that may be an influence of his work with spirituals.

Source: First edition (Galaxy Music Corporation, 1951).

35. Wright: *We are the music makers*

Reginal Wright (b. 1976) is a composer, conductor, and educator based in Texas. He is regularly commissioned by school, college, and professional choirs, and is a sought-after clinician in both gospel and classical genres. As an educator, he has earned many awards over his career and has performed throughout Europe and the United States. In 2008, Wright was appointed as Head Choral Director at Mansfield High School, Texas, and his choirs are consistent sweepstakes winners in both concert and sight-reading contests. *We are the music makers* was commissioned by the University of Nebraska–Lincoln's Glenn Korff School of Music to celebrate the 100th anniversary of the birth of George Walker (1922–2018). The request was for a piece that may be learned in only a few hours of rehearsal, if necessary. Wright's uplifting setting displays his signature lyrical style with accessible ranges and contemporary harmonies.